Facts About the Spider Monkey

By Lisa Strattin

© 2020 Lisa Strattin

FREE BOOK

FREE FOR ALL SUBSCRIBERS

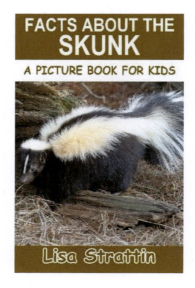

LisaStrattin.com/Subscribe-Here

BOX SET

- **FACTS ABOUT THE POISON DART FROGS**
- **FACTS ABOUT THE THREE TOED SLOTH**
  - **FACTS ABOUT THE RED PANDA**
  - **FACTS ABOUT THE SEAHORSE**
  - **FACTS ABOUT THE PLATYPUS**
  - **FACTS ABOUT THE REINDEER**
  - **FACTS ABOUT THE PANTHER**
- **FACTS ABOUT THE SIBERIAN HUSKY**

LisaStrattin.com/BookBundle

Facts for Kids Picture Books by Lisa Strattin

Sign Up for New Release Emails Here

LisaStrattin.com/subscribe-here

COVER IMAGE

https://www.flickr.com/photos/proyectoasis/40668191372/

ADDITIONAL IMAGES

ONE IMAGE PUBLIC DOMAIN

https://www.flickr.com/photos/threefingers/2590794168/

https://www.flickr.com/photos/guldem/24609059477/

https://www.flickr.com/photos/kittysfotos/11114780004/

https://www.flickr.com/photos/digitalsextant/3442861439/

https://www.flickr.com/photos/eye1/3185562151/

https://www.flickr.com/photos/goingslo/18425537072/

https://www.flickr.com/photos/76526364@N06/13561563625/

https://www.flickr.com/photos/31267353@N03/28043478819/

https://www.flickr.com/photos/proyectoasis/48241860571/

Contents

INTRODUCTION

The Spider Monkey is a good-sized monkey that can be found living in South America, from Brazil to Southern Mexico.

CHARACTERISTICS

The Spider Monkeys are supposedly named after spiders because of the way they hang in the trees. They spread out with both feet and both hands on different branches.

This makes the monkey look like a spider web!

They can also hang from their tail!

APPEARANCE

The Spider Monkey looks just like other monkeys. With two arms, legs and a tail; they are able to grab tree branches with each of these and swing all over the trees where they live.

Their fur can be black, brown, white, grey and even a combination of these colors.

FAMILY LIFE

Spider Monkeys live in a family group that breaks up during the day when looking for food. There can be as few as 10 monkeys or as many as 30 in this group.

Females will choose a mate and have one baby at a time every three to four years. She is pregnant for about 7 months. The baby stays with the mother, usually hanging on tightly to her tummy or her back until the baby is at least six months old. This is to make it easy to feed the baby and to keep it safe from predators.

Unlike many other primates, the males will stay with their original group while the females move away to join or start another one when they are old enough.

LIFE SPAN

A Spider Monkey can live to be 25 years of age!

SIZE

The Spider Monkey is a monkey that grows to be 20' tall, with as much as an additional 20" in the length of the tail!

One generally weighs between 15 to 25 pounds.

HABITAT

The Spider Monkey lives in the rainforest and tropical jungle. Because they live in the trees, this is the natural habitat for them. This is also where they find the food they like to eat.

Rainforests are moist, so the food for them is plentiful in this environment.

DIET

The Spider Monkey likes to eat berries. leaves and fruits from the trees where they live. Occasionally they will eat bugs and small reptiles.

ENEMIES

The Spider Monkey is hunted by Jaguars and Crocodiles! Since these animals live in the rainforest with them, the monkeys have to always be on the lookout for these predators.

SUITABILITY AS PETS

Spider Monkeys are kept as pets all around the world. However, in some areas they are considered an exotic pet. This means that you might need a special license to keep one. Be sure to check your local laws before buying one as a pet to make sure it is legal to have one.

They are considered endangered because so many are being taken out of their native jungle habitat.

More and more of them are bred in captivity. Therefore, you might be able to find a reputable breeder who can provide you with a baby Spider Monkey that would make a very good pet. This would also allow you to have one without endangering the native populations of Spider Monkeys in the world.

COLOR ME

COLOR ME

COLOR ME

COLOR ME

COLOR ME

COLOR ME

COLOR ME

COLOR ME

COLOR ME

COLOR ME

Please leave me a review here:

LisaStrattin.com/Review-Vol-366

For more Kindle Downloads Visit Lisa Strattin Author Page on Amazon Author Central

amazon.com/author/lisastrattin

To see upcoming titles, visit my website at LisaStrattin.com– most books available on Kindle!

LisaStrattin.com

FREE BOOK

FOR ALL SUBSCRIBERS – SIGN UP NOW

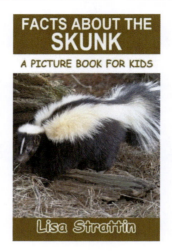

LisaStrattin.com/Subscribe-Here

LisaStrattin.com/Facebook

LisaStrattin.com/Youtube

Printed in Great Britain
by Amazon